FOR MOTHER
a gift of love

Edited by Helen Exley

EXLEY

In the same series:
For Father, with love
Love, a Celebration
Marriage, a Keepsake
Love, a Keepsake

Also edited by Helen Exley:
Grandmas and Grandpas
To Mom
To Dad
Happy Birthday (you poor old wreck)
Cats (and other crazy cuddlies)
What it's like to be me

Published by Exley Publications Ltd,
16 Chalk Hill, Watford, Herts,
United Kingdom WD1 4BN.
Selection and design © Exley Publications Ltd 1983
First published in Great Britain 1983
Distributed in the United States by Interbook Inc, 14895 E.
14th Street, Suite 370, San Leandro, CA 94577, USA.

Printed and bound in Hungary

British Library Cataloguing in Publication Data
For mother, a gift of love.
   1. Mother – Literary collections
   2. English literature
I. Exley, Helen
820.8'0354   PR1111.M/

ISBN 0-905521-76-5

To my own dear mother, with all my love

Agnes 1987

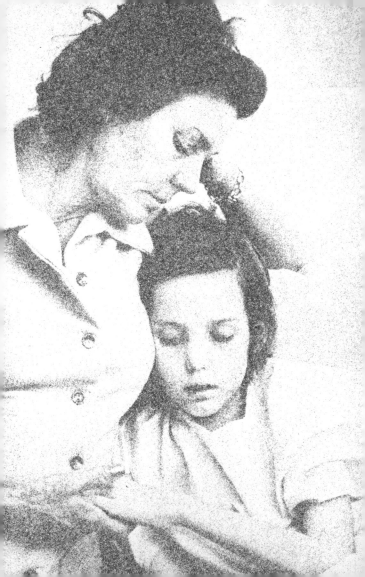

Mother, I love you so.
Said the child, I love you more than I know.
She laid her head on her mother's arm,
And the love between them kept them warm.

Stevie Smith

HAEC ORNAMENTA SUNT MEA

Cornelia, the mother of the Gracchi, once
entertained a woman from Campania at her house.
Since the woman made a great show of her jewels,
which were among the most beautiful of the time,

Cornelia detained her in conversation until her children came home from school. Then, pointing to her children, she said, "These are my jewels.'

from Valerius Maximus (1st century)

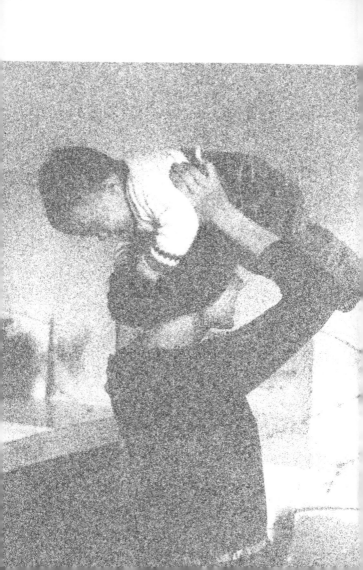

Children, look into those eyes, listen to the dear voice, notice the feeling of even a single touch that is bestowed upon you by that gentle hand! Make much of it while yet you have that most precious of all good gifts, – a loving mother. Read the unfathomable love of those eyes; the kind anxiety of that tone and look, however slight your pain. In after life you may have friends, fond, dear friends, but never will you have again the inexpressible love and gentleness lavished upon you, which none but mother bestows.

Thomas Babington Macaulay

TO MY SON

Son, I am powerless to protect you though
My heart for yours beats ever anxiously,
Blind through piteous darkness you must go,
And find with a new vision lights I see.
If it might ease you I would bear again
All the old suffering that I too have known,
All sickness, terror, and the spirit's pain,
But you, alas, must make those three your own.
Yes, though I beat away a thousand fears
And forge your armour without flaw or chink,
And though I batter Heaven with my prayers,
Yet from a self-filled cup of grief you drink.
Oh, son of woman, since I gave you breath
You walk alone through life to face your death.

Dorothea Eastwood

Every man, for the sake of the great blessed Mother in Heaven, and for the love of his own little mother on earth, should handle all womankind gently, and hold them in all honour.

Alfred Lord Tennyson

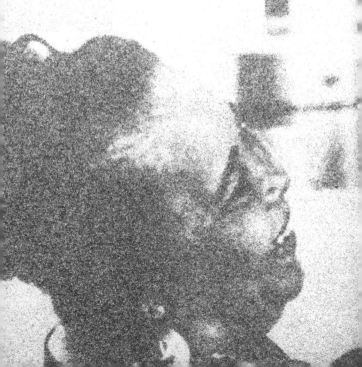

I would desire for a friend the son who never resisted the tears of his mother.

Lacretalle

A man loves his sweetheart the most, his wife the best, but his mother the longest.

Irish proverb

Dear Mother. Never listens to an argument, never lets logic interfere with the warm impulses of her heart. Singing around the house, a girl's voice still, a bird's heart.
Capricious, unpredictable, generous, tactless, stubborn, unreasonable, and lovable mother.

Maurice Wiggin

"The woman with happiness inside her" – this was the way of describing a pregnant woman.

Old Chinese

All that I am or hope to be, I owe to my angel mother.

Abraham Lincoln

My mother was the making of me. She was so true and so sure of me, I felt that I had someone to live for – someone I must not disappoint. The memory of my mother will always be a blessing to me.

Thomas A. Edison

Children do not know how their parents love them,
and they never will till the grave closes over those
parents, or till they have children of their own.

Edmund Vance Cooke

BECAUSE SHE IS A MOTHER

She broke the bread into fragments and gave them to the children, who ate with avidity.

"She hath kept none for herself," grumbled the Sergeant.

"Because she is not hungry," said a soldier.

"Because she is a mother," said the Sergeant.

Victor Hugo

THE HEROISM OF THE AVERAGE MOTHER

How many thousands of heroines there must be now, of whom we shall never know. But still they are there. They sow in secret the seed of which we pluck the flower, and eat the fruit, and know not that we pass the sower daily in the streets.

One form of heroism – the most common, and yet the least remembered of all – namely, the heroism of the average mother. Ah! When I think of that broad fact, I gather hope again for poor humanity; and this dark world looks bright – this diseased world looks wholesome to me once more – because, whatever else it is not full of, it is at least full of mothers.

Charles Kingsley

MOTHER COURAGE

In the wake of every evil inflicted by man or nature
come the women, gathering what can be salvaged,
the distraught and injured children, the lost, the
dispossessed, the fragments of a broken society.
They stoop across every battlefield, seeking for their
own. They tear at blocks of stone tumbled by
earthquake, blackened by fire. They build among
the olive trees or the desert sand.

Out of destruction they piece together small areas
of safety, letting fragments stand as symbols of a
whole. Here is a house, patched out of cardboard;
here is a kitchen, stocked with rusted cans. Here is a
cradle in a nest of rags. The earth erupts, the typhoon
sweeps away a clutch of villages, the causes rage
across the landscape, the bitter wire divides. But the
women crouch beside their fires and hide the
children in their shawls. They have suffered too
much in making life to let it go so easily; they cannot
think in cold statistics or see the death of any child as
a necessity.

Pamela Brown

MOTHER'S DAY

The ritual of the flowers was a small thing; but it served to give continuity to our lives and to remind us for one day to be nicer, sweeter, more thoughtful of a mother who could always shame us to tears any time we slipped and "acted ugly".

Mother's Day has turned into something of a joke for the sophisticated. It is a day that brings out gritty editorials and comments on "commercialism". But, like millions of others, I still mark Mother's Day. I send the "cute" cards and sometimes a plant or box of chocolates or a special note. Any occasion depends, after all, on the spirit with which one celebrates it; like Christmas, either a glory or a horror.

Liz Smith, from "The Mother Book"

A GIFT FOR MAMA

. . . I have been worrying for weeks now about what to give my mother for Mother's Day. For most people this is a modest problem, solved by the purchase of a box of chocolates. For me, however, Mother's Day represents an annual challenge to do the impossible — find a gift that will make neither Mama nor me feel terrible.

Expensive gifts are out, because they make Mama feel terrible. "This is awful," she says, examining an apron. "I feel just terrible. You shouldn't have spent the money on me." Inexpensive presents please Mama, but they make *me* feel terrible.

There is always the danger a gift given to Mama will bounce swiftly back to the giver. If I buy her something to wear, she perceives in an instant that it could be let in here, let out there, and it would fit me perfectly. If I give her a plant, she cuts off the top for me to take home and root in a glass of water.

If I give her something edible, she wants me to stay for lunch and eat it.

Papa, a sensible man, long ago stopped trying to shop for Mama. Instead, on Mother's Day, her birthday and other appropriate occasions, he composes for her a short epic poem in which he tells of their meeting, courtship and subsequent marriage. After nearly thirty years of poems, Papa sometimes worries that the edge of his poetic inspiration has dulled, but Mama doesn't complain. She comes into the room while he is struggling over a gift poem and says, "It doesn't have to rhyme, as long as it's from the heart."

This year, finally, I think I too have found a painless gift for Mama. I am going to give her a magazine article, unrhymed but from the heart, in which I wish her "Happy Mother's Day", and tell her that there's nothing Papa or I could ever buy, find or make for her that would be half good enough, anyway.

Helene Melyan, from an article in 'The Oregonian'

EPILOGUE TO MOTHER'S DAY, WHICH IS TO BE PUBLISHED ON ANY DAY BUT MOTHER'S DAY

Mothers! Mothers! It was visions of mothers that
    had been relentlessly haunting me,
Wherever I turned I saw misty mothers sitting
    around taunting me.
It was battalions of irritated specters that blanched
    my face and gave me this dull and luster-lack eye,
Night and day I was surrounded by mothers, from
    Mrs. Whistler, Senior, to Mrs. Dionne and from
    Yale the mother of men to Niobe and the mother
    of the Gracchi.
I resented this supernatural visitation, these are not
    the dark ages, these are the days of modernity,
I wilted before this intrusion of miasmic maternity.
Mothers, I cried, oh myriads of mothers, I can
    stand it no longer, what can I do for you?
Do you want me to have you exorcised, do you
    want me to pray for you, do you want me to say
    Boo for you?
I know you are major figures in history's Who's
    Whom,
But I wish you would go away because your
    company is flattering but I would rather have
    your room.
Then they replied in hollow chorus,
We have thought of something that we want to
    have published but we can't write so you will
    have to write it for us,

And if you write it we will leave you alone,
And if you don't write it we will haunt you brain
from skull and flesh from bone,
So I acquiesced and the ghastly horde dictated to
me and I wrote it,
And a promise is a promise and an army of ghostly
mothers is an army of ghostly mothers, so I
quote it:—
M is for the preliminary million-dollar advertising
appropriation,
O means that she is always white-haired,
bespectacled and at least eighty-five years old,
T is for Telegraph message number 31B which
contains a tastefully blended expression of
sentiment and congratulation,
H is for the coast-to-coast questionnaire which
proved conclusively that seven-and-one-half
citizens out of every ten with incomes of $5,000 a
year or better would rather have their mother
than gold.
E is for Elephants which everybody is very glad
didn't sit down on their mothers,
R is for Rosemary which is for Remembrance of the
fact that a mother is one thing that you will never
have more than one of,
Put them all together and before you can say H.
Wellington Carruthers, they spell what
everybody who loves their mother only once a
year and then only at the instigation of the
Chamber of Commerce is a son of.

Ogden Nash

Few of us, if any, are so fortunate as to be able to look back to any time in our lives with regret, because we were too dutiful, gentle, kind, and generous to our good mothers. On the contrary, most of us if not all, have heartaches, when too late, we wish we were more loving, more dutiful, more thoughtful in every way, to give pleasure, when we could; so that this day is intended to bring to our mind a more active thought, to make the lives of our mothers happier and brighter, and to see where we can improve on the past.

Very often our good mothers hunger and yearn for the loving thoughts which every true mother cherishes. Often a good mother's life is filled with emptiness: because of love never shown, and letters from the absent son and daughter that never come. And yet no man or woman is too poor or too busy to remember this devoted parent.

Mother's Day is to remind us of our duty before it is too late.

L. L. Loan, on the first Mother's Day

All mothers are rich when they love their children.
There are no poor mothers, no ugly ones, no old
  ones.
Their love is always the most beautiful of the joys.
And when they seem most sad, it needs but a kiss
  which they receive or give to turn all their tears
  into stars...

Maurice Maeterlinck

FROM A LETTER TO HIS MOTHER

. . . What was best was your wishing to see me. Of course you know that I feel that too . . . But because that cannot be, we are still no further away than we ever were and when the pain to see you comes, I don't let it hurt and I don't kill it either for it is the sweetest pain I feel. If sons will go off and marry, or be war correspondents, or managers, it doesn't mean that Home is any the less Home. You can't wipe out history by changing the name of a boulevard, as somebody once said about the French . . . You will never know how much I love you all and you must never give up trying to comprehend it. God bless you and keep you, and my love to you every minute and always.

Richard Harding Davis

I remember the flash of insight I had in 1940 as I sat talking to a small delegation that had come to ask me to address a women's congress. I had my baby on my lap, and as we talked I recalled my psychology professor's explanation of why women are less productive than men. He had referred to a letter written by Harriet Beecher Stowe in which she said that she had in mind to write a novel about slavery, but the baby cried so much. It suddenly occurred to me that it would have been much more plausible if she had said "but the baby smiles so much." It is not that women have less impulse than men to be creative and productive. But through the ages having children, for women who wanted children, has been so satisfying that it has taken some special circumstance – spinsterhood, barrenness, or widowhood – to let women give their whole minds to other work.

Margaret Mead

There is an enduring tenderness in the love of a mother to a son that transcends all other affections of the heart. It is neither to be chilled by selfishness, nor daunted by danger, nor weakened by worthlessness, nor stifled by ingratitude. She will sacrifice every comfort to his convenience; she will surrender every pleasure to his enjoyment; she will glory in his fame and exalt in his prosperity; and if adversity overtake him, he will be the dearer to her by misfortune; and if disgrace settle upon his name, she will still love and cherish him; and if all the world beside cast him off, she will be all the world to him.

Washington Irving

SHE WORKS AT TASKS

She works at tasks
Requiring no especial skill,
Yet making their demands,
Hard to fulfil,
Demands on time and patience
And the capricious will.

Grease blears the gaze
Of water cooling in the bowl
And films her wrists and hands;
Toil takes its toll
Of strength, drains light and music
From the air and numbs the soul;

Or surely would
Except her love re-makes all things,
And every trivial chore,
Transmuted, brings
A sacramental joy
And, while she works, she sings.

Vernon Scannell

It was reported that a 123-pound woman, Mrs. Maxwell Rogers, lifted one end of a 3,600lb. (1.60 tons) stationwagon which, after the collapse of a jack, had fallen on top of her son at Tampa, Florida, on 24 April 1960. She cracked some vertebrae.

From "The Guinness Book of Records"

In the eyes of its mother every beetle is a gazelle.

Moroccan proverb

When you havva no babies, you havva nothing.

Italian immigrant woman

A CLASSIC

When the son leaves home to start his freshman year at college, his doting mother gives him two cashmere sweaters as going-away presents. Wanting to show his appreciation, the boy comes home for Thanksgiving wearing one of the sweaters.

The mother greets him at the door. She takes a long, anxious look and says: "What's the matter? The other sweater you didn't like?"

Liz Smith

At eighty-eight the mother of the Parrish children was still working in Hollywood as an extra. "She won't take a taxi, too expensive, and we took her car away from her a few years ago," said Parrish. "So my brother, who is a senior vice-president for Coca-Cola, will be in conference and the phone will ring.

'Gordon, will you drive me over to Universal?' And he drops everything and does it."

You see, it's never easy to say no to a genuine stage mother.

From "Growing Up in Hollywood" by Robert Parrish

No matter how old a mother is she watches her middle-aged children for signs of improvement.

Florida Scott-Maxwell

the worst to be said
   about mothers
   is that they
   are prone
     to give
     kisses
   of con-
   grat-
   u-
   lation
which make you feel
   like a battleship
   on which someone
   is breaking
      a bottle

Norman Mailer

What was locked in that extremity of expression
that I so loved as a child? When the grown-ups
became annoyed with our childish fights and
shrieks and sent us out of the house yelling, "Go
play in the traffic!" Why did I feel deeply secure,
certain of their undying love? Was it that by their
yelling, their faces puffing red, their fingers
pointing dramatically toward the door, their hateful
words screaming out at the tops of their lungs, that
I knew how much they loved us? Yes, it was that.
But it was more. I sensed, I now know, that they,
by their own expression, acknowledged the devil in
us all, established their toleration for the reality of
our humanness. "You are my hell on earth, my
endless burden!" the mother shrieks at the child she
patently adores. And the child, if not the neighbors,
hears the silent addition: "my reason for staying
alive."

Jane Lazarre in "Village Voice"

. . . We were poor, but we refused to be pitiful, and although we were Black, we felt precious. . . We never felt like losers. We were the exact opposite of the Marilyn Monroe syndrome, the beautiful golden goddess who because of her bad childhood and sense of worthlessness was never able to feel like a goddess. We were little black pickaninnies, but because of the way we were treated by our family, we felt very favored. I remember how at Christmas time Zella would call all the creditors and tell them she wouldn't be able to pay them because she had to buy something for her kids. She always made it clear to us and to everybody else that we were something special and to be indulged. Some families have the wherewithal, but they act as if it were some kind of betrayal of parental responsibilities to indulge their kids. Her feeling was, "I want these children to know we care about them, that we give them the best we have. . ."

Florynce Kennedy

FROM A LETTER TO HER DAUGHTER

I can remember the exact moment you were
conceived and shouted aloud and exulted with
perhaps the most perfect feeling I've ever had. It was
under the trees in the middle of the day during the
war when I was camp following. Your dad had a
couple of hours off and we had gone for a drive. And
I said – that's my new baby. And it's always going to
love the sky through the trees and the birds and the
smell of grass and earth and busy insects and rising
trunks and togetherness. And so it has happened.

Of course I thought I could never love my second
baby as much as I had loved my first, but from the
moment I held you in my arms I had a surge of
mother love that outweighed any feelings of doubt.

It has been the same with my grandchildren. I
adored Lincoln with all my heart. Then I thought, I
will try, but I can't love Dalton just as much. Well, of
course, he went into my heart with such violence that
he is there on top, boots and all. (No, flat feet and all).

When Sue was on the way, I decided to try my best
not to discriminate – but, what do you know, from

the first moment my heart expanded to take her in. Each passing year she gives more to me and I love her more – which of course is impossible – because I loved her with all my heart all the time.

Then came Jeff – now I was sure he was an also-ran. Well, he is such a charmer and so gentle and, well just Jeff, that I can't help it – he occupies all my heart, just like the others.

Oh, dear – then came Gareth, the last. Well, he just looked so adorable and well, I just loved him. He was a difficult baby and for a few months I felt sorry for him because he cried a lot, and so I loved him more to make up for what seemed wrong. Now he is the most humorous strong active loving child you could imagine.

I know you don't like to say 'all my love', but I do. I use it with discrimination, but it certainly embraces both my children, both my children-in-law and my five grandchildren. I have other loves, for relations and friends, but this all-pervasive love that draws us together is limited to these few, and still embraces my own Pop and Mom.

Marion Garretty

WALKING AWAY

It is eighteen years ago, almost to the day –
A sunny day with the leaves just turning,
The touch-lines new-ruled – since I watched you play
Your first game of football, then, like a satellite
Wrenched from its orbit, go drifting away

Behind a scatter of boys, I can see
You walking away from me towards the school
With the pathos of a half-fledged thing set free
Into a wilderness, the gait of one
Who finds no path where the path should be.

That hesitant figure, eddying away
Like a winged seed loosened from its parent stem,
Has something I never quite grasp to convey
About nature's give-and-take – the small, the
    scorching
Ordeals which fire one's irresolute clay.

I have had worse partings, but none that so Gnaws at
    my mind still. Perhaps it is roughly
Saying what God alone could perfectly show –
How selfhood begins with a walking away,
And love is proved in the letting go.

C. Day Lewis

THE MOTHER

There will be a singing in your heart,
There will be a rapture in your eyes;
You will be a woman set apart,
You will be so wonderful and wise.
You will sleep, and when from dreams you start
As of one that wakes in Paradise,
There will be a singing in your heart,
There will be a rapture in your eyes.

There will be a moaning in your heart,
There will be an anguish in your eyes,
You will see your dearest ones depart,
You will hear their quivering good-byes.
Yours will be the heart-ache and the smart,
Tears that scald and lonely sacrifice;
There will be a moaning in your heart,
There will be an anguish in your eyes.

There will come a glory in your eyes,
There will come a peace within your heart;
Sitting 'neath the quiet evening skies,
Time will dry the tear and dull the smart.
You will know that you have played your part;
Yours shall be the love that never dies:
You, with Heaven's peace within your heart,
You, with God's own glory in your eyes.

Robert Service

PIANO

Softly, in the dusk, a woman is singing to me;
Taking me back down the vista of years, till I see
A child sitting under the piano, in the boom of the
  tingling strings
And pressing the small, poised feet of a mother who
  smiles as she sings.

In spite of myself, the insidious mastery of song
Betrays me back, till the heart of me weeps to belong
To the old Sunday evenings at home, with winter
  outside
And hymns in the cosy parlour, the tinkling piano
  our guide.

So now it is vain for the singer to burst into clamour
With the great black piano appassionato. The
   glamour
Of childish days is upon me, my manhood is cast
Down in the flood of remembrance, I weep like a
   child for the past.

D. H. Lawrence

THE CHAIR IN WHICH YOU'VE SAT

The chair in which you've sat's not just a chair
nor the table at which you've eaten just a table
nor the window that you've looked from just a
    window.
All these have now a patina of your
body and mind, a kind of ghostly glow
which haloes them a little, though invisible.

Iain Crichton Smith

As years ago we carried to your knees
The tales and treasures of eventful days,
Knowing no deed too humble for your praise,
Nor any gift too trivial to please,
So still we bring, with older smiles and tears,
What gifts we may, to claim the old, dear right;
Your faith, beyond the silence and the night,
Your love still close and watching through the
    years.

Kathleen Norris

TO A MOTHER

Know, I am never far from you, I bear you
inwardly as you bore me – as intimately too
and as my flesh is of your own
and our early mesh, woven one
so you are still my own
and everything about you, home,
the features, eyes, the hands, your entire form
are the past, present and to come,
the familiarity, the ease
of my living, and my peace.

Pamela Chalkley

MOTHER MACHREE

There's a spot in me heart which no colleen may
    own,
There's a depth in me soul never sounded or known,
There's a place in my memory, my life, that you fill,
No other can take it, no one ever will.

Sure I love the dear silver that shines in your hair
And the brow that's all furrowed, and wrinkled with
    care.
I kiss the dear fingers, so toil-worn for me,
Oh, God bless you and keep you, Mother Machree!

Every sorrow or care in the dear days, gone by,
Was made bright by the light of the smile in your eye
Like a candle that's set in a window at night,
Your fond love has cheered me and guided me right.

Rida Johnson Young

Sonnets are full of love, and this my tome
   Has many sonnets: so here now shall be
   One sonnet more, a loving sonnet from me
To her whose heart is my heart's quiet home,
   To my first Love, my Mother on whose knee
I learnt love-lore that is not troublesome:
   Whose service is my special dignity
And she my lodestar while I go and come.
And so because you love, and because
   I love you, Mother, I have woven a wreath
Of rhymes wherewith to crown your honoured name:
   In you not fourscore years can dim the flame
Of love, whose blessed glow transcends the laws
   Of time and change and mortal life and death.

Christina G. Rossetti

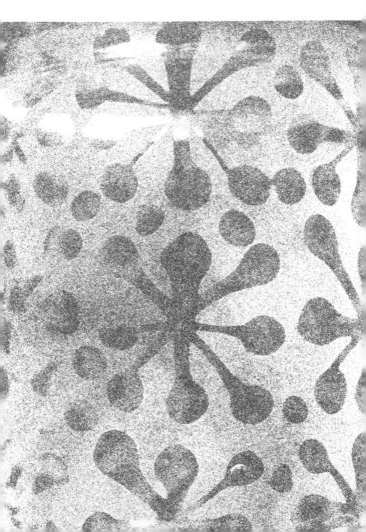

A LONG PARTING

You have been long from me
and I have tried to treat your absence as normality,
and live as once I did before you came;
but now your hands hold mine
and all the years are gone
and all the hidden pain,
and I'm complete again.

Charlotte Gray

MOTHER O' MINE

If I were hanged on the highest hill,
   Mother o' mine, O mother o' mine!
I know whose love would follow me still,
   Mother o' mine, O mother o' mine!
If I were drowned in the deepest sea,
   Mother o' mine, O mother o' mine!

I know whose tears would come down to me,
   Mother o' mine, O mother o' mine!
If I were damned by body and soul,
I know whose prayers would make me whole,
   Mother o' mine, O mother o' mine!

Rudyard Kipling

Hey kids! Remember me?
I'm the lady with the Christmas tree.
I'm the lady with the beard and sack . . .

Waved you off and hugged you back.
Packed your bags and waited up . . .

Bought you a bicycle. Bought you a pup.

Kissed you better and blew your noses.
Bottled you jam and picked you roses.

Legs gone shaky; stuck in a chair.
Not too sure about when or where.
Don't quite know how I got like this . . .

Send me a letter . . .

Send me a kiss.

Pamela Brown

You will have the road gate open, the front door ajar
The kettle boiling and a table set
By the window looking out at the sycamores –
And your loving heart lying in wait

For me coming up among the poplar trees.
You'll know my breathing and my walk
And it will be a summer evening on those roads
Lonely with leaves of thought.

We will be choked with the grief of things growing,
The silence of dark-green air
Life too rich – the nettles, docks and thistles
All answering the prodigal's prayer.

You will know I am coming though I send no word
For you were lover who could tell
A man's thoughts – my thoughts – though I hid them –
Through you I knew Woman and did not fear her
    spell.

Patrick Kavanagh

...Fifty-four years of love and tenderness and crossness and devotion and unswerving loyalty. Without her I could only have achieved a quarter of what I have achieved, not only in terms of success and career, but in terms of personal happiness. We have quarrelled, often violently, over the years, but she has never stood between me and my life, never tried to hold me too tightly, always let me go free. For a woman of her strength of character this was truly remarkable. There was no fear in her except for me. She was a great woman to whom I owe the whole of my life.

Noël Coward

. . . Children, children,
Why do we ever have children?
They only grow up and they leave one day
And they blame us for taking their dreams away,
And the houses are empty, the nurseries forlorn,
These were beautiful places when they were born.
Children, children,
What can you say about children?
Who knows where their childhood ends,
Or when it ends,
Just why you drift apart.
I only know that they never leave your heart.

Hal Shaper

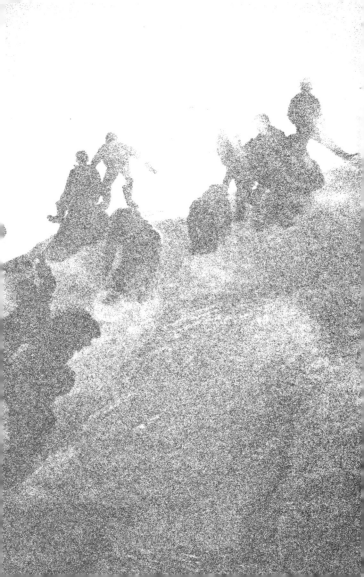

ACKNOWLEDGEMENTS: The publishers gratefully acknowledge permission to reproduce copyright material. Every effort has been made to trace copyright holders, but in a few cases this has proved impossible. The publishers would be interested to hear from any copyright holders not here acknowledged. NOEL COWARD, extract from *The Life of Noel Coward* by Cole Lesley, published by Jonathan Cape. Reprinted by permission of the publishers and the Cole Lesley Estate; IAIN CRICHTON SMITH, "The Chair in which You've Sat", Reprinted from *Love Poems & Elegies* by permission of Victor Gollancz Ltd; C. DAY LEWIS, "Walking Away" from *The Gate* published by Jonathan Cape. Reprinted by permission of A. D. Peters Ltd and the Executors of the Estate of C. Day Lewis; DOROTHEA EASTWOOD, "To My Son". Reprinted by permission of Hugo Eastwood; ELIZABETH GOUDGE, "To a Mother" from *A Book of Faith*, published by Hodder & Stoughton Ltd; GUINNESS SUPERLATIVES, extract from The Guinness Book of Records. Reprinted by permission of the publishers; PATRICK KAVANAGH, "You will have the road gate open". Reprinted from *"The Collected Poems of Patrick Kavanagh"* by permission of the publishers, Martin Brian & O. Keeffe Ltd, and Mrs Katherine Kavanagh; FLORYNCE KENNEDY, "We were poor but we..." from *Color Me Flo*; RUDYARD KIPLING, "Mother O'Mine" from *"The Light that Failed"*. Reprinted by permission of The National Trust; D. H. LAWRENCE, "Piano", from *The Complete Poems* published by William Heinemann Ltd. Reprinted by permission of Laurence Pollinger Ltd and the Estate of Frieda Lawrence Ravagli and Viking Penguin of N.Y.; JANE LAZARRE, extract. Reprinted by permission of Jane Lazarre © Village Voice February 23rd 1976; MAURICE MAETERLINCK by kind permission of George, Allen and Unwin; NORMAN MAILER, "The worst to be said..." from *Deaths for the Ladies (and other Disasters)*. Reprinted by permission of the author and the author's agent, Scott Heredith Literary Agency, Inc., 845 Third Avenue, New York, New York 10022; MARGARET MEAD, extract from *Blackberry Winter: My earlier years*. Reprinted by permission of Angus & Robertson UK Ltd and William Morrow & Co. Inc; HELENE MELYAN, "A Gift for Mama". Reprinted by permission of The Oregonian, Portland, Oregon and Reader's Digest Association, New York; OGDEN NASH, "Epilogue to Mother's Day, which is to be published on any day but Mother's Day". Reprinted by permission of Curtis Brown Ltd, London on behalf of the Estate of Ogden Nash and Little, Brown and Company; KATHLEEN NORRIS, "As years ago we carried to your knees"; ROBERT PARRISH, extract from *Growing up in Hollywood*, published by The Bodley Head. Reprinted by permission of the publishers and Robert Parrish; VERNON SCANNELL, "She works at tasks" from *The Loving Game* published by Robson Books Ltd. Reprinted by permission of the publishers; FLORIDA SCOTT-MAXWELL, from "Revelations: Diaries of Women", edited by Mary Jane Moffat and Charlotte Painter; ROBERT SERVICE, "The Mother" from *Rhymes of a Rolling Stone*. Reprinted by permission of Ernest Benn, McGraw-Hill Ryerson Ltd, Toronto, Dodd Mead & Company Inc.; HAL SHAPER, "Children". Music by Cyril Ornadel from the musical version of *"Great Expectations"* and reprinted by permission of The Sparta Florida Music Group Ltd and Aviva Music Ltd; LIZ SMITH, two extracts from *The Mother Book* published by Granada. Reprinted by permission of the publishers and Doubleday; STEVIE SMITH, "Human Affection" from *The Collected Poems* published by Allen Lane. Reprinted by permission of James MacGibbon, executor of the Stevie Smith Estate; MAURICE WIGGIN, "Dear Mother. Never listens to an argument" from *Compliments* by G. Polickman. Reprinted by permission of George Allen & Unwin; RIDA JOHNSON YOUNG, "Mother Machree", © 1910 renewed. Warner Brothers Inc, all rights reserved.

PHOTOGRAPHS AND ILLUSTRATIONS:
NICHOLAS BATTYE: illustrating extract by Florynce Kennedy; MARK COLLINS: illustrating "Mother Machree"; JOHN DE VISSER: illustrating lyrics by Hal Shaper and "Because she is a Mother"; MARY EVANS PICTURE LIBRARY: illustrating extracts by Robert Parrish and Liz Smith; DALTON EXLEY who recreated the front cover illustration from a design in *Art Nouveau Designs in Color* by Mucha et al 1974 published by DOVER PUBLICATIONS INC. N.Y.; RICHARD EXLEY illustrating "A Gift for Mama", "Hey kids! Remember me?", "Sonnets are full of love", poem by Norman Mailer, "Mother Courage", "From a Letter to her Daughter" and "To a Mother"; JOHN HEDGECOE: photograph of figure shadows taken from above and illustrating extract by Jane Lazarre, reprinted by permission of John Hedgecoe and Mitchell Beazley International; SYLVESTER JACOBS: illustrating "As years ago..." and extract by T. B. Macaulay, Charlotte Grey and Maurice Maeterlinck; ANDREWS/SOURCE: illustrating "The Mother", "Mother o' Mine", the letter by Richard Harding Davies and extract by Margaret Mead; HENRY MOORE: illustrating "The Heroism of the Average Mother"; PICASSO: illustrating "To My Son" from Stuttgart, Staatsgalarie and "She Works at Tasks" reprinted by permission of Spadem; POPPERFOTO: Photograph of Muhammad Ali; CLAIRE SCHWOB: illustrating extract by Maurice Wiggin; MURRAY SUMNER: illustrating "The Chair in which You've Sat"; DENNIS THORPE: illustrating "Haec Ornamenta Sunt Mea"; VAN GOGH: illustrating "Walking Away" from the Van Gogh Collection, Amsterdam; GEORGE WEDDING: illustrating "Mother, I love you so".

Other gift books produced by Exley Publications

For Father, £4.95. $7.95. A neat little book handsomely
bound in soft suedel. A companion volume to *For Mother, a
gift of love*, this thoughtfully compiled collection of verse and
prose is designed to show fathers how much they are
appreciated.
Love, a Celebration, £4.95. $7.95. In the same series as this
but with a burgundy suedel cover. Writers and poets old and
new have captured the feeling of being in love, in this very
personal collection.
Grandmas & Grandpas, £4.50. $7.95. Children are close
to grandparents, and this book reflects that warmth. "A
Grandma is old on the outside and young on the inside." An
endearing book for grandparents. Our most popular book!
To Dad, £4.50. $7.95. Another in our series written and
illustrated entirely by children "Fathers are always right, and
even if they're not right, they're never actually wrong." Dads
will love this book — it's so true to life!
To Mum, £4.50. **To Mom**, $7.95. "When I'm sad she
patches me up with laughter." A thoughtful, joyous gift for
Mother entirely created by children. Get it for Mother's Day
or her birthday.
Happy Birthday (you poor old wreck), £4.50. $7.95.
This is a cheering book for all those old people over 21 who
keep moaning about their age. It points out both the
disadvantages ("when you're 50 you start getting crincals")
and the advantages ("Look on the brighter side of being bald.
At least you don't have to wash your hair any more").
Old is… great! £3.25, $5.95. A wicked book of cartoons
which pokes fun at youth and revels in the first silver hairs of
middle age. "Extremely funny" (Daily Telegraph).

United Kingdom
Free catalogue available on request. Books may be ordered
through your bookshop, or by post from Exley Publications,
16 Chalk Hill, Watford, Herts, United Kingdom WD1 4BN.
Please add 95p as a contribution to postage and packing.

United States
Distributed in the United States by Interbook Inc, 14895 E.
14th Street, Suite 370, San Leandro, CA 94577, USA.